THE IRIDESCENCE OF BIRDS

A Book About Henri Matisse

PATRICIA MACLACHLAN

pictures by
HADLEY HOOPER

A NEAL PORTER BOOK
ROARING BROOK PRESS
NEW YORK

If you were a boy named Henri Matisse who lived
in a dreary town in northern France where the skies were gray

And the days were cold

And you wanted color and light
And sun,

And your mother, to brighten your days,

Painted plates to hang on the walls

With pictures of meadows and trees,

Rivers
and birds,

And she let you mix the colors of paint—

Yellow and red,

Red and blue,
Blue and yellow—

And let you arrange the fruit and flowers
She brought from the market—

Pears and oranges in a bowl
On a tablecloth,

And flowers in a blue vase—

And in the town people wove silks

With colors

All tangled,
One color

Next to the other
Next to the other,

And your mother put red rugs on the walls of the house

And on the dirt parlor floor

So all the world looked red,

And you raised pigeons,

Watching their sharp eyes
And red feet,

And their colors that changed with the light
As they moved

That your mother called iridescence,

Would it be a surprise that you
grew up to be a fine painter

Who painted red rooms

And flowers that danced on green stems

And fruit in a bowl
On a blue and white tablecloth?

Would it be a surprise that you became
A fine painter who painted

Light
and
Movement

And the iridescence of birds?

"My mother loved everything I did."
—Henri Matisse

Why do painters paint what they do? Do they paint what they see or what they remember? The great painter Henri Matisse's life story may have some answers.

Henri Matisse was born in December of 1869 in a far northern, gray mill town in France. There was little sun and natural light, but Henri grew up with color and painted plates that his mother brought into the leaky cottage. She put colorful red rugs on the beaten dirt floors and on the walls. His father gave him pigeons, and Henri watched their colors change as they moved.

He began to paint as a young man when he was in the hospital and his mother brought him a paint set.

"I got my sense of color from my mother," he once said.

After studying art in Paris, Matisse began to paint with strong, bright colors and bold forms and patterns. It became his own style, and he was part of a group of painters known as the Fauves, the French name for "wild beasts." They painted about their feelings and emotions rather than exactly how things looked. Matisse had great success and influenced the course of modern art. In his old age he began to work with paper cutouts, but he also worked with pencil or charcoal when he became too ill to paint.

He always loved birds and kept them his whole life. He had many artist friends, and before he died at age eighty-four in 1954 he gave his beloved birds to his friend, the artist Pablo Picasso.

His paintings, sculptures, and cutouts can be seen in museums all over the world.

In writing this book I think I found the answer to the question that inspired it. Henri Matisse painted what he saw *and* what he remembered—he painted his feelings and he painted his childhood.

—Patricia MacLachlan

I've always loved the problem-solving and research aspects of illustration, but I've never been able to invest myself as completely as I did with this book. I spent months looking at reproductions of Henri Matisse's paintings, drawings, cutouts, and prints. I studied his line, his composition, and his color. I researched and imagined the patterns he might have seen growing up in the textile town of Bohain-en-Vermandois. Using Google maps I was able to piece together what his street and childhood home looked like.

I thought about his work just before sleep and, as the deadline approached, as soon as I woke up. It was a total immersion and a total luxury.

I decided to try relief printing, which forced me to simplify my shapes and allowed me to focus on the color and composition. I cut the characters and backgrounds out of stiff foam and cardboard, inked them up, made prints, and scanned the results into Photoshop. The approach felt right.

And after working on several pages, my floor and desk were covered in odd, colorful shapes that reminded me of a photo I had seen of Matisse's floor after what must have been a busy session of cutouts!

—Hadley Hooper

SOME BOOKS ON HENRI MATISSE YOU MIGHT WANT TO READ

Goldman Rubin, Susan. *Matisse: Dance for Joy.* San Francisco: Chronicle Books, 2008.

Johnson, Keesia and Jane O'Connor. *Henri Matisse: Drawing with Scissors.* New York: Grosset & Dunlap, 2002.

Le Tord, Bijou. *A Bird or Two: A Story About Henri Matisse.* Grand Rapids: Eerdmans Books for Young Readers, 1999.

Welton, Jude. *Henri Matisse: Artists in Their Time.* New York: Franklin Watts, 2002.

For Henri Matisse's mother, Anna Heloise Matisse, who brought color to his life —P.M.

For my mother who, like Matisse's, encouraged creativity —H.H.

Text copyright © 2014 by Patricia MacLachlan
Illustrations © 2014 by Hadley Hooper
A Neal Porter Book
Published by Roaring Brook Press
Roaring Brook Press is a division of Holtzbrinck Publishing Holdings Limited Partnership
120 Broadway, New York, NY 10271
The art for this book was created using a combination of relief printmaking and digital techniques.
mackids.com

Library of Congress Cataloging-in-Publication Data
MacLachlan, Patricia, author.
    The iridescence of birds / Patricia MacLachlan ; illustrated by Hadley
Hooper. — First edition.
        pages cm
    "A Neal Porter book."
    ISBN 978-1-59643-948-1 (hardcover)
1. Matisse, Henri, 1869–1954—Juvenile literature. 2.
Painters—France—Biography—Juvenile literature. I. Hooper, Hadley,
illustrator. II. Title.
    ND553.M37M25 2014
    759.4—dc23
    [B]
                                                    2013044238

Roaring Brook Press books may be purchased for business or promotional use. For information on bulk purchases
please contact Macmillan Corporate and Premium Sales Department at (800) 221-7945 x5442
or by email at specialmarkets@macmillan.com.

First edition 2014
Book design by Jennifer Browne
Printed in China by Toppan Leefung Printing Ltd., Dongguan City, Guangdong Province

9 10 8